D0463060

# Tacos
## QUESADILLAS & BURRITOS

# Tacos
## QUESADILLAS & BURRITOS

**LAURA WASHBURN**
**Photography by Isobel Wield**

RYLAND
PETERS
& SMALL

LONDON NEW YORK

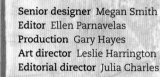

**Senior designer** Megan Smith
**Editor** Ellen Parnavelas
**Production** Gary Hayes
**Art director** Leslie Harrington
**Editorial director** Julia Charles

**Food stylist** Lizzie Harris
**Prop stylist** Lucy Harvey

First published in 2012 by
Ryland Peters & Small
20–21 Jockey's Fields,
London WC1R 4BW
and
Ryland Peters & Small, Inc.
519 Broadway, 5th Floor
New York NY10012

www.rylandpeters.com

Text © Laura Washburn 2012
Design and photographs
© Ryland Peters & Small 2012

10 9 8 7 6 5 4 3 2 1

ISBN: 978-1-84975-215-2

The author's moral rights
have been asserted. All rights
reserved. No part of this
publication may be reproduced,
stored in a retrieval system
or transmitted in any form
or by any means, electronic,
mechanical, photocopying or
otherwise, without the prior
permission of the publisher.

A CIP record for this book is
available from the British Library.

US Library of Congress
cataloging-in publication data
has been applied for.

Printed and bound in China.

**Note:** Use small (15 cm/6 inch)
corn or flour tortillas to make
tacos and large (25 cm/10 inch)
flour tortillas to make burritos
and quesadillas.

# Contents

# Introduction

Simply put, a taco is a filling wrapped in a tortilla. It is street food, it is fast food, but it is healthy food. Where I grew up, in Southern California, tacos and burritos were such a common sight that they were even on the school lunch menu. It is only recently, however, that the taco craze has reached beyond the Mexican border.

The tacos of my childhood were not always as high-quality as they are now. The filling was predictably ordinary and they were encased in mass-produced corn shells, intended to be crispy but usually soggy from the greasy fillings often served. Tacos have come a long way since then, and what is now on offer is a better representation of the real thing.

In Mexico, tacos are generally served as a light meal or snack, either as a quick mid-morning bite, a pre-dinner appetizer or late-night dish. Quesadillas and burritos are also made from different fillings wrapped in tortillas and can be eaten at any time of day.

A tortilla meal is not really a knife and fork affair, so the recipes in this book are intended for informal dining. While tacos are best made to order and eaten almost immediately, burritos and quesadillas can be prepared more easily in

advance. Burrito fillings, in particular, are ideal for freezing in individual portions, making them the perfect candidate for lunchboxes.

All of the recipes in this book are ideal for entertaining. For a taco buffet, otherwise known as a 'taquisa', simply prepare several fillings of your choice as well as several salsas. Accompany these with an array of fresh toppings, such as chopped fresh coriander/cilantro, spring onions/scallions and tomatoes, grated cheese, a bowl of sour cream and some warmed tortillas. Tacos can be accompanied by rice and refried beans, and dessert can be as simple as sliced tropical fruit or lime sorbet topped with fresh mint leaves.

The beauty of tacos, burritos and quesadillas is that they are so easy to prepare. Fillings can be mixed and matched and served with many different sauces and salsas. And, because the trend is really catching on, many specialist ingredients are now readily available. In Mexico, fillings are based on regional specialities, but tacos are so versatile that this practice can be extended to almost anywhere in the world. With a bit of imagination, there is almost certainly a fabulous taco filling in your fridge right now. The key is to use what you have already available. Use the inspiring recipes in this book as a springboard for refining your inner taco-making potential.

Buen provecho!

# Tacos

Mexican street food is often chargrilled, so cook the steaks over an open flame for a truly authentic flavour. These tacos are very simple to prepare and, after one bite, you'll be hooked.

# Lime-marinated rib eye tacos with red onion relish

. . . . . . . . . . . . . . . . . . .

juice of 3 limes
1 teaspoon ground cumin
1 teaspoon fine sea salt
1 kg/2 lb 4 oz. thick boneless rib eye steaks
1 tablespoon vegetable oil
8–12 flour tortillas, warmed

**FOR THE RELISH**
2 red onions, thinly sliced
1 small bunch fresh coriander/cilantro, finely chopped
juice of ½ orange
juice of 2 limes
1 tablespoon white wine vinegar or cider vinegar
½ teaspoon fine sea salt

**TO SERVE**
Guacamole (see page 60)
thinly sliced tomatoes

**SERVES 4–6**

To prepare the relish, put the onions, coriander/cilantro, orange and lime juice, vinegar and salt in a small bowl. Mix well to combine, cover and leave to marinate in the refrigerator for at least 4 hours, but preferably overnight. Return to room temperature before serving.

To prepare the steaks, combine the lime juice, cumin and salt in a shallow dish large enough to hold the steaks in a single layer. Add the steaks and toss to coat evenly. Cover and leave to marinate in the refrigerator for at least 4 hours, but preferably overnight. Return to room temperature before cooking.

Heat the oil in a stovetop grill pan/griddle set over high heat or preheat the barbecue. Cook the steaks for 4–5 minutes on each side depending on the thickness of the steaks. Season lightly with salt and let stand for 5 minutes before slicing thinly on the diagonal.

To serve, spread each tortilla with a thin layer of Guacamole. Add a generous helping of steak and top with a spoonful of onion relish. Serve immediately with sliced tomatoes and extra Guacamole on the side.

In my childhood, this was the only taco filling I ever knew. A well-seasoned ground beef filling is always a winner.

# Ground beef tacos

. . . . . . . . . . . . . . . . . .

2 tablespoons vegetable oil

1 small onion, grated

2 generous teaspoons ground cumin

½ teaspoon dried chilli/hot pepper flakes

1 tablespoon dried oregano

2 garlic cloves, crushed

1 fresh green chilli/chile, very finely chopped

500 g/1 lb 2 oz. beef mince/ ground beef

1 teaspoon fine sea salt

juice of ½ lime

a small handful of chopped fresh coriander/cilantro

6–12 flour tortillas, warmed

**TO SERVE**

grated Cheddar or Monterey Jack cheese

crisp lettuce, thinly sliced

Guacamole (see page 60)

Pico de Gallo (see page 63)

**SERVES 4–6**

Heat the oil in a frying pan/skillet set over medium–high heat. Add the onion, cumin, dried chilli/hot pepper flakes and oregano and cook for 1–2 minutes, stirring often, until aromatic. Add the garlic and fresh chilli/chile and cook for 1 minute. Add the beef and salt, and mix to combine and break up the beef. Cook for 8–10 minutes, stirring occasionally, until well browned.

Taste and adjust the seasoning. Add the lime juice and coriander/ cilantro and stir well.

To serve, put a generous helping of beef in the middle of each tortilla. Top with grated cheese, lettuce and spoonfuls of Guacamole and Pico de Gallo. Serve immediately with extra Pico de Gallo on the side.

Spicy pineapple salsa perfectly complements the richness of the roasted pork belly in this recipe. The salsa is best made fresh, but prepare the meat a day ahead for extra flavour.

# Marinated pork belly
# tacos with pineapple salsa

. . . . . . . . . . . . . . . . . . . .

400 ml/1½ cups pineapple juice
2 tablespoons white wine vinegar
   or cider vinegar
1 teaspoon chipotle chilli/chili
   powder
¼ teaspoon dried chilli/ hot
   pepper flakes
1 kg/2 lb 4 oz. pork belly, sliced
2 teaspoons fine sea salt
freshly ground black pepper
6–12 flour tortillas, warmed

**FOR THE SALSA**
1 small pineapple, finely diced
1 small fresh green chilli/chile,
   finely chopped
½ red onion, finely chopped
a small bunch fresh coriander/
   cilantro, finely chopped
juice of 1 lime

**SERVES 4–6**

To prepare the pork, combine the pineapple juice, vinegar, chilli/chili powder and dried chilli/hot pepper flakes in a heatproof dish large enough to hold the pork slices in a single layer. Add the pork and toss to coat evenly. Season with salt and a good grinding of black pepper to taste. Cover and leave to marinate in the refrigerator until needed, but preferably overnight. Return to room temperature before cooking.

Preheat the oven to 200ºC (400ºF) Gas 6.

Cover the pork with foil and roast in the preheated oven for 1–1½ hours, until the meat is tender.

Meanwhile, prepare the salsa. Put the pineapple, chilli/chile, onion, coriander/cilantro and lime juice in a small bowl. Mix well to combine and set aside for at least 1 hour.

To serve, shred the pork into small pieces and mix well with any remaining juices from the pan. Put a generous helping of pork in the middle of each tortilla and top with a spoonful of the Pineapple Salsa. Serve immediately with extra salsa on the side.

A reminder that taco fillings need not be complex, these tacos are filled with simply cooked chicken. For an even easier option, feel free to shred a ready-roasted chicken instead of cooking your own. This simple recipe is the perfect opportunity to serve up with a variety of delicious salsas and sides such as Guacamole or Roasted Tomato Salsa.

# Shredded chicken tacos

· · · · · · · · · · · · · · · · · · ·

600 g/1 lb 5 oz. boneless, skinless
   chicken
chicken or vegetable stock,
   or water, as required
10–12 flour tortillas, warmed
200 g/2 cups feta cheese or queso
   fresco, crumbled
fine sea salt and freshly ground
   black pepper

**TO SERVE**
Roasted Tomato Salsa
   (see page 60)
Guacamole (see page 60)
sprigs of fresh coriander/cilantro
hot sauce (such as Tabasco)
halved limes

**SERVES 3–4**

Put the chicken in a saucepan and add enough stock or water to cover. If using water or unseasoned stock, season with salt.

Bring to the boil over medium heat, then cover and simmer gently for 30–40 minutes until cooked through and tender. Remove the chicken from the pan and let cool slightly, then shred using your hands or two forks. Taste and adjust the seasoning.

To serve, put a generous helping of the shredded chicken in the centre of each tortilla and sprinkle over a handful of crumbled cheese. Top with spoonfuls of Roasted Tomato Salsa and Guacamole and a sprig of fresh coriander/cilantro. Serve immediately with extra Roasted Tomato Salsa and Guacamole, any hot sauce and halved limes for squeezing.

Rajas simply means strips of pepper. Roast chicken works best in this recipe but if oven space, or time, is an issue, you can sauté the chicken on the stovetop instead (see Variation below).

# Chipotle chicken & rajas tacos

. . . . . . . . . . . . . . . . . . . .

500 g/1 lb 2 oz. boneless, skinless chicken, thinly sliced
2 teaspoons ground cumin
1 teaspoon chipotle chilli/chili powder
2 teaspoons fine sea salt
2 tablespoons vegetable oil
6–8 corn or flour tortillas, warmed

**FOR THE RAJAS**
1 red bell pepper, thinly sliced
1 yellow bell pepper, thinly sliced
2 tablespoons vegetable oil
2 garlic cloves, crushed
1 teaspoon dried oregano
fine sea salt

**TO SERVE**
sour cream
freshly ground black pepper
hot sauce (such as Tabasco)

**SERVES 4**

Preheat the oven to 180°C (350°F) Gas 4.

To prepare the rajas, put the peppers in a large roasting pan. Add the oil, garlic, oregano and salt and toss well. Spread evenly in the pan and roast in the preheated oven for 20–30 minutes until the peppers begin to char. Remove from the oven and set aside until needed. Do not turn off the oven.

Put the chicken in a roasting pan. Add the cumin, chilli/chili powder salt and oil and toss well. Spread in an even layer and roast for 15–20 minutes until browned and cooked through.

To serve, put a generous helping of sliced chicken in the middle of each tortilla. Top with rajas, a spoonful of sour cream and a good grinding of black pepper. Serve immediately with extra sour cream and any hot sauce on the side.

**VARIATION** To sauté the chicken, heat the oil in a large frying pan/skillet. When hot, add the chicken and cook for 5–10 minutes, stirring occasionally, until well browned and cooked through.

Asparagus is not a traditional Mexican ingredient, but the shape of the spears makes an attractive filling. These are more elegant than the average taco and are perfect for entertaining.

# Lamb & asparagus tacos

700 g/1 lb 9 oz. lean lamb, sliced
(leg is best)
2–4 tablespoons vegetable oil
1–2 teaspoons ground cumin
500 g/1 lb 2 oz. asparagus spears,
tough ends removed
juice of ½ lemon
8–10 corn tortillas, warmed
150 g/1½ cups feta cheese
or queso fresco, crumbled
Roasted Tomato Salsa
(see page 60), to serve
fine sea salt and freshly ground
black pepper

SERVES 4

Put the lamb slices in a shallow dish and drizzle with 1–2 tablespoons of the oil. Sprinkle over the cumin and rub in evenly. Cover and leave to marinate in the refrigerator for at least 30 minutes, but preferably overnight. Return to room temperature before cooking.

To prepare the asparagus, heat the remaining oil over high heat in a large frying pan/skillet and add as many asparagus spears as will fit in a single layer – you may need to work in batches. Cook for 3–4 minutes on each side, without stirring, to char the asparagus. Transfer to a plate and repeat to cook the remaining asparagus. Before removing the last batch from the pan, squeeze over the lemon juice, cook for about 30 seconds then pour the pan juices over all of the cooked asparagus. Toss to coat evenly, season with salt and pepper to taste and set aside.

Preheat a stovetop grill pan/griddle over high heat. When hot, add the lamb slices and cook for 2–3 minutes on each side to sear. Remove from the heat, season with salt and let stand for a few minutes.

To serve, put a generous helping of sliced lamb in the middle of each warmed tortilla and sprinkle over the crumbled cheese. Top with a few asparagus spears and a spoonful of the Roasted Tomato Salsa. Serve immediately with extra Roasted Tomato Salsa on the side.

Tangy, fruity salsas are ideal with seafood. This one may look innocent but the fresh chilli/chile gives it quite a kick.

# Seafood tacos
## with mango-kiwi salsa

. . . . . . . . . . . . . . . . . .

2 tablespoons lime juice
a small bunch fresh coriander/
   cilantro, finely chopped
1 teaspoon ground cumin
1 teaspoon ancho chilli/chili
   powder
½ teaspoon fine sea salt
750 g/1 lb 10 oz. raw prawns/
   shrimp, shelled
2–4 tablespoons vegetable oil
8–10 corn tortillas, warmed
sour cream, to serve
freshly ground black pepper

**FOR THE SALSA**
1 mango, flesh finely diced
3 kiwis, flesh finely diced
1 small red onion, finely chopped
1 fresh green chilli/chile, very
   finely chopped
a few sprigs fresh coriander/
   cilantro, finely chopped
 juice of 1 lime

**SERVES 4**

To prepare the prawns/shrimp, combine the lime juice, coriander/cilantro, cumin, chilli/chili powder and salt in a bowl. Add the prawns/shrimp and toss well to coat evenly. Cover and set aside until needed.

To prepare the salsa, put the mango, kiwis, onion, chilli/chile, coriander/cilantro and lime juice in a small bowl. Mix well to combine and set aside until needed.

Heat the oil in a large frying pan/skillet set over high heat. Add as many prawns/shrimp as will fit in a single layer – you may need to work in batches. Cook for about 5 minutes until pink and cooked through. Season with pepper to taste.

To serve, put a generous helping of the prawns/shrimp in the middle of each tortilla, top with a spoonful of the Mango-Kiwi Salsa and sour cream. Serve immediately with extra sour cream and Mango-Kiwi Salsa on the side.

Traditional fish tacos are coated in batter and deep-fried but this is a healthier version.

# Orange-marinated fish tacos with chilli cream

......................

juice of 1 orange

2 teaspoons ground cumin

½ teaspoon ancho chilli/chili powder

a pinch of fine sea salt

800 g/1 lb 12 oz. boneless skinless fish fillets, such as tilapia

flour, for dusting

2–3 tablespoons vegetable oil

8 flour or corn tortillas, warmed

**FOR THE CHILLI CREAM**

6 tablespoons sour cream

2 tablespoons plain yogurt

1 small fresh red chilli/chile, very finely chopped

a pinch of fine sea salt

a small bunch of fresh coriander/cilantro, finely chopped

**TO SERVE**

1 quantity Baja Slaw (see page 59)

lime wedges

**SERVES 4**

To prepare the fish, combine the orange juice, cumin, chilli/chili powder and salt in a shallow dish large enough to hold the fish in a single layer. Add the fish and toss well to coat evenly. Cover and leave to marinate in the refrigerator until needed, but preferably overnight. Return to room temperature before cooking.

To prepare the chilli/chile cream, put the sour cream, yogurt, chilli/chile, salt and coriander/cilantro in a bowl. Mix well, cover and set aside until needed.

Remove the fish from the marinade and pat dry with paper towels. Put the flour on a plate, add a pinch of salt and mix well.

Heat the oil in a frying pan/skillet set over high heat. Dip each fish fillet in the seasoned flour on both sides, shake off the excess and fry for 2–4 minutes on each side, until browned and crisp on the edges and cooked through. Transfer to paper towels to drain.

To serve, arrange a small mound of Baja Slaw in the middle of each tortilla. Top with pieces of the cooked fish and add a spoonful of Chilli Cream. Serve immediately with lime wedges and extra Chilli Cream on the side.

This makes a nice change from some of the meatier fillings, so is ideal for a vegetarian meal or a light snack.

# Ancho-roasted butternut squash tacos

......................

1 large onion, halved and sliced
4 tablespoons vegetable oil
2 teaspoons ground cumin
2 teaspoons dried oregano
2 teaspoons ancho chilli/chili powder
1 teaspoon fine sea salt
a good pinch of ground cinnamon
1.2 kg/2 lb 12 oz. butternut squash, peeled and cubed
8–12 corn or flour tortillas, warmed

**TO SERVE**
sour cream
sprigs of fresh coriander/cilantro
Guacamole (see page 60)
hot sauce (such as Tabasco)
lemon wedges

**SERVES 4–6**

Preheat the oven to 220°C (425°F) Gas 7.

To prepare the squash, combine the onion slices, oil, cumin, oregano, chilli/chile powder, salt and cinnamon in a large bowl. Add the squash and toss well to coat evenly.

Spread the spiced squash mixture on a baking sheet large enough to hold it in a single layer. Roast in the preheated oven for 25–35 minutes until well browned.

To serve, put a generous helping of squash in the middle of each tortilla. Top with a spoonful of sour cream and scatter over a few sprigs of fresh coriander/cilantro. Serve immediately with Guacamole, any hot sauce and lemon wedges on the side for squeezing.

A satisfying and unusual way to serve potatoes, these tacos are good morning, noon or night. The spicing here is deliberately mild, but if you like it fiery, add a finely chopped fresh chilli/chile to the potatoes before roasting.

# Potato tacos

....................

1 generous teaspoon ground cumin

1 generous teaspoon ancho chilli/chile powder or sweet smoked paprika

4–5 tablespoons vegetable oil

1.25 kg/2 lb 12 oz. potatoes, unpeeled and diced

1–2 teaspoons fine sea salt

10–12 corn tortillas, warmed

200 g/2 cups feta cheese or queso fresco, crumbled

a small bunch of fresh coriander/cilantro, finely chopped

**SERVES 4**

Preheat the oven to 220°C (425°F) Gas 7.

To prepare the potatoes, put the cumin, chilli/chili powder and 2 tablespoons of the oil in a large mixing bowl. Add the potatoes and toss well to coat evenly. Arrange the potatoes in a single layer on a baking sheet – you may need to use two baking sheets. Drizzle over the remaining oil and sprinkle liberally with salt.

Roast the potatoes in the preheated oven for 10 minutes, then stir to brown on all sides. Return to the oven and cook for a further 10 minutes, or until browned and tender.

To serve, put a generous helping of potatoes in the middle of each tortilla. Top with crumbled cheese and scatter over some chopped coriander/cilantro. Serve immediately.

**VARIATION** For breakfast tacos, top the potatoes with a spoonful of scrambled eggs and top with cheese and salsa.

Grilling the courgettes/zucchini and corn cobs gives them a smoky, chargrilled taste, which can be achieved using either a stovetop grill pan/griddle or a barbecue.

# Mixed vegetable tacos
## with chipotle-lime mayo

. . . . . . . . . . . . . . . . . . .

1 kg/2 lb 4 oz. courgettes/zucchini,
   halved and sliced
vegetable oil
2 corn cobs
fine sea salt
½ teaspoon ground cumin
10–12 small corn or flour tortillas,
   warmed
Pico de Gallo (see page 63),
   to serve

**FOR THE MAYO**
6–8 generous tablespoons
   mayonnaise
juice of 1 lime
½ teaspoon chipotle chilli/chili
   powder
freshly ground black pepper

**SERVES 4**

To prepare the Chipotle-Lime Mayo, combine the mayonnaise, lime juice, chilli/chili powder and a good grinding of black pepper in a small bowl. Mix well to combine. Taste and adjust the seasoning then cover and refrigerate until needed.

Put the courgettes/zucchini in a mixing bowl and drizzle with oil. Mix well so they are lightly coated. Heat a stovetop grill pan/griddle until hot. Cook the courgette/zucchini slices for 3–5 minutes on each side until charred. Rub the corn cobs with oil, then cook for 10–15 minutes, turning often, until charred all over. Set aside.

Dice the charred courgette/zucchini slices and place in a shallow dish. Scrape the charred kernels from the corn cobs and add to the courgettes/zucchini. Add the cumin. Season with salt and mix well.

To serve, put a generous helping of the vegetable mixture in the middle of each tortilla. Top with a spoonful of Chipotle-lime Mayo and Pico de Gallo and serve immediately.

# Burritos

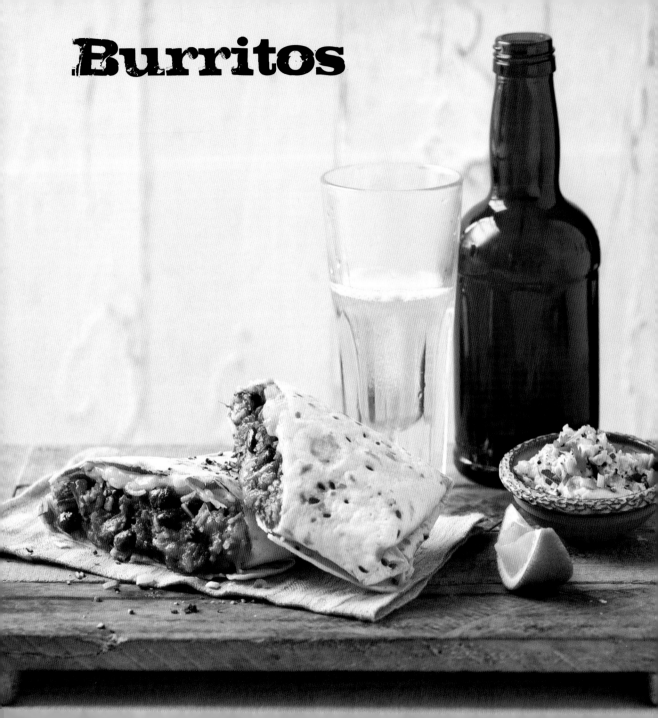

Hearty and substantial, these beef, bean and rice burritos are a meal in themselves and will satisfy the most demanding of hungers. Guacamole on the side is the perfect accompaniment.

# Beer-braised beef burrito

......................

400 g/14 oz. braising beef,
   cut into large chunks
1 large onion, finely chopped
3 garlic cloves, finely chopped
a pinch of ground allspice
1 teaspoon ground cumin
1 teaspoon dried oregano
1 generous teaspoon fine sea salt
freshly ground black pepper
250 ml/1 cup beer
400 ml/1½ cups passata (Italian
   sieved tomatoes)
2 ancho chillies/chiles in adobo
   sauce, finely chopped, plus
   1 teaspoon of adobo sauce
400-g/14-oz. can black beans,
   drained
300 g/1½ cups cooked rice
4–6 large flour tortillas
150 g/1½ cups grated Cheddar
   or Monterey Jack cheese
Guacamole (see page 60), to serve

**SERVES 4**

Combine the beef, onion, garlic, allspice, cumin, oregano, salt and pepper in a large casserole dish. Add the beer and enough water to cover by about 1 cm/½ inch. Set over high heat and bring to the boil, then cover and let simmer for 1½–2 hours until the meat is tender.

Strain the meat and transfer it to a chopping board. Return the onion to the casserole dish and reserve 500 ml/2 cups of the broth.

Shred the beef using your hands, or two forks then return to the pot with the onion. Add the passata, ancho chillies/chiles with adobo sauce, beans, 250 ml/1 cup of the reserved broth and the rice. Stir well.

Cook over medium heat for 15–20 minutes until slightly reduced and thickened. Taste and adjust the seasoning. If the mixture is too thick, add a bit more of the reserved broth, or water.

Preheat the oven to 200°C (400°F) Gas 6.

Divide the beef filling between the tortillas and sprinkle with grated cheese. Fold in the sides of each tortilla to cover the filling, then roll up to enclose. Place the filled tortillas seam-side down on a greased baking sheet or in a shallow dish.

Cover with foil and bake in the preheated oven for 10–15 minutes just to warm through and melt the cheese. Serve hot with Guacamole on the side.

A fantastic way to start the day, breakfast burritos can just as easily be eaten for lunch or a light supper. The ingredients can be varied according to what is on hand. Try adding sautéed mushrooms, chopped fresh tomatoes or even crispy bacon.

# Breakfast burrito

· · · · · · · · · · · · · · · · · · · ·

5 large eggs
1 large potato, cooked and diced
1 fresh red or green chilli/chile,
    finely chopped
2–3 spring onions/scallions,
    finely chopped
a small bunch fresh coriander/
    cilantro, finely chopped
1 teaspoon fine sea salt
2 tablespoons unsalted butter
75 g/scant 1 cup grated Cheddar
    or Monterey Jack cheese
2 large flour tortillas
1 avocado, thinly sliced
Pico de Gallo (see page 63),
    to serve

**SERVES 2**

Put the eggs in a large bowl and whisk well. Stir in the diced potato, chilli/chile, spring onions/scallions, coriander/cilantro and salt.

Melt the butter in a large frying pan or skillet. Add the egg mixture and cook, stirring often, until the eggs are just set. Stir in the cheese, cook for 1 minute then transfer to a plate.

To serve, divide the egg mixture between warmed tortillas and top with avocado slices. Fold the bottom up over most of the filling, then fold over the sides, overlapping to enclose the filling but leaving the burrito open at one end. Serve immediately with Pico de Gallo on the side.

Chorizo adds another layer of spice to these delicious burritos, so any variety will work well here.

# Chorizo, bean & pepper burrito

· · · · · · · · · · · · · · · · · · · ·

1 tablespoon vegetable oil
1 large onion, diced
1 red or yellow bell pepper, diced
2 garlic cloves, crushed
1 teaspoon dried oregano
½ teaspoon dried chilli/hot
   pepper flakes
225 g/8 oz. chorizo, diced
400-g/14-oz. can chopped
   tomatoes
400-g/14-oz. can haricot or
   cannellini beans, drained
6 large flour tortillas
250 g/2½ cups grated Cheddar
   or Monterey Jack cheese
fine sea salt and freshly ground
   black pepper
sour cream, to serve

**SERVES 6**

Preheat the oven to 200°C (400°F) Gas 6.

Heat the oil in a large frying pan/skillet set over medium–high heat. Add the onion and pepper and cook for 5–8 minutes, stirring occasionally, until browned. Add the garlic, oregano, dried chilli/hot pepper flakes and chorizo and cook for 1–2 minutes. Add the tomatoes, beans, 4 tablespoons water and season with salt. Cook for about 15 minutes, stirring occasionally, until thickened. Taste and adjust the seasoning.

Divide the filling between the tortillas and sprinkle with grated cheese. Fold in the sides of each tortilla to cover the filling, then roll up to enclose. Place the filled tortillas seam-side down on a greased baking sheet or in a shallow dish.

Cover with foil and bake in the preheated oven for 10–15 minutes just to warm through and melt the cheese. Serve hot with sour cream on the side.

This classic Mexican recipe is a mouth watering combination of pork simmered in orange juice with a warm blend of spices.

# Orange-braised pork burrito

· · · · · · · · · · · · · · · · · · · ·

1.2 kg/2 lb 12 oz. pork, with fat, shoulder or leg, cut into chunks
juice of 3–4 oranges
2 garlic cloves, crushed
1 teaspoon fine sea salt
a pinch of ground allspice
1 teaspoon ground cumin
300 g/1½ cups cooked rice
4–6 large flour tortillas
180 g/scant 2 cups grated Cheddar or Monterey Jack cheese
freshly ground black pepper

**FOR THE PURÉE**
3 dried ancho chillies/chiles, deseeded
1 onion, coarsely chopped
¼ cup cider vinegar
½ teaspoon dried oregano
½ teaspoon ground cumin
1 teaspoon fine sea salt

**SERVES 4–6**

Preheat the oven to 200°C (400°F) Gas 6.

Combine the pork, orange juice, garlic, salt, allspice and cumin in a large casserole dish. Set over high heat and bring to the boil. Lower the heat and simmer for 1½-2 hours, uncovered, until tender. Let the meat cool in the cooking liquid, cover and refrigerate until needed.

To prepare the chilli/chile purée, soak the chillies/chiles in boiling water for 15 minutes. Remove the chillies/chiles and reserve the liquid. Remove the stems from the chillies/chiles and put them in a food processor with the onion, vinegar, oregano, cumin, salt and 375 ml/1½ cups of the soaking liquid. Blend until smooth.

Remove the pork from the casserole dish and reserve the cooking liquid. Using your hands, or two forks, separate the meat from the fat and shred the meat. Remove any fat from the surface of the cooking liquid and return it to the casserole dish with the shredded meat. Stir in the rice and chilli/chile purée. Simmer for 10 minutes. Taste and adjust the seasoning and stir in the coriander/cilantro.

Divide the pork mixture between the tortillas and sprinkle with grated cheese. Fold in the sides of each tortilla to cover the filling, then roll up. Place the filled tortillas seam-side down on a greased baking sheet or in a shallow dish. Cover with foil and bake in the preheated oven for 10–15 minutes just to warm through and melt the cheese. Serve hot.

A mole is a deliciously spicy Mexican sauce. In this recipe, it is made from ready-made mole paste because it can be labour-intensive to make and difficult to source the ingredients.

# Chicken mole burrito

500 g/1 lb 2 oz. boneless skinless
   chicken
chicken or vegetable stock,
   or water, as required
1 tablespoon vegetable oil
1 large onion, finely chopped
200 g/1 cup good-quality mole
   poblano paste
300 g/1½ cups cooked rice
400-g/14-oz. can pinto beans,
   drained
4–6 large flour tortillas
180 g/scant 2 cups grated Cheddar
   or Monterey Jack cheese
fine sea salt
freshly ground black pepper

SERVES 4–6

Put the chicken in a large saucepan and add enough stock or water to cover. If using water or unseasoned stock, season with salt.

Bring to the boil over medium heat, then cover and simmer gently for 30–40 minutes until cooked through and tender. Remove the chicken from the pan and let cool slightly, then shred using your hands or two forks. Taste and adjust the seasoning.

Heat the oil in a saucepan set over medium-high heat. Add the onion and cook for about 5–8 minutes, stirring occasionally, until golden. Stir in the mole paste and dilute according to the package instructions, using a little stock, or water. Cook for 1–2 minutes further. Add the shredded chicken, rice and beans and mix well. Simmer over low heat for 10–15 minutes.

Divide the chicken mixture between the tortillas and sprinkle with grated cheese. Fold in the sides of each tortilla to cover the filling, then roll up to enclose. Place the filled tortillas seam-side down on a greased baking sheet or in a shallow dish. Cover with foil and bake in the preheated oven for 10–15 minutes just to warm through and melt the cheese. Serve hot.

**These delicious breakfast burritos are a particularly great way to start the day, but they are fantastic eaten at any time.**

# Adobo, bean & cheese burrito

· · · · · · · · · · · · · · · · · · · ·

2 tablespoons vegetable oil

1 large onion

2 teaspoons ground cumin

2 teaspoons dried oregano

3 garlic cloves, finely chopped

1–3 ancho chillies/chiles in adobo
   sauce, finely chopped

2 x 400-g/14-oz. cans black beans,
   drained

230-g/8-oz. can chopped tomatoes

250 ml/1 cup chicken or vegetable
   stock, or water

2 teaspoons fine sea salt

a pinch of sugar

200g/1 cup cooked rice

4–6 large flour tortillas

180 g/scant 2 cups grated Cheddar
   or Monterey Jack cheese

sprigs of fresh coriander/cilantro,
   to serve

freshly ground black pepper

**SERVES 4–6**

Preheat the oven to 200°C (400°F) Gas 6.

Heat the oil in a large saucepan set over medium–high heat. Add the onion, cumin and oregano and cook for 5–8 minutes, stirring occasionally, until golden. Add the garlic and chillies/chiles and cook, stirring often, for 1 minute further.

Add the beans, tomatoes, stock or water, salt and sugar and mix well. Bring to the boil and simmer over low heat for 10–15 minutes. Stir in the rice, then taste and adjust the seasoning.

Divide the bean mixture between the tortillas and sprinkle with grated cheese. Fold in the sides of each tortilla to cover the filling, then roll up to enclose. Place the filled tortillas seam-side down on a greased baking sheet or in a shallow dish. Cover with foil and bake in the preheated oven for 10–15 minutes just to warm through and melt the cheese. Serve hot, topped with sprigs of fresh coriander/cilantro.

# Quesadillas

This filling is a real crowd pleaser and the seasoning
can be varied to keep it as mild, or as spicy, as desired.

# Pepper beef quesadilla

· · · · · · · · · · · · · · · · ·

2 tablespoons vegetable oil
1 onion, diced
1 red bell pepper, diced
1 yellow bell pepper, diced
1 teaspoon ground cumin
1 teaspoon dried oregano
½ teaspoon paprika
1 fresh red or green chilli/chile
2 garlic cloves, crushed
450 g/1 lb beef mince/ground beef
1 teaspoon fine sea salt
220 g/1 cup canned chopped
   tomatoes
8 large flour tortillas
150 g/1½ cups grated Cheddar or
   Monterey Jack cheese

**TO SERVE**
sour cream
spring onions/scallions, sliced
diced tomatoes
pitted black olives, sliced

**SERVES 4-6**

Preheat the oven to 120°C (250°F) Gas ½.

Heat 1 tablespoon of the oil in a frying pan/skillet set over
medium–high heat. Add the onion and peppers and cook
for 5–8 minutes, stirring occasionally, until golden. Add the
cumin, oregano, paprika, chilli/chile and garlic and cook for
1 minute further. Add the beef and salt and cook for 5 minutes
until browned. Stir in the tomatoes and simmer until slightly
reduced and thickened. Taste and adjust the seasoning.

To assemble the quesadillas, spread a quarter of the beef
mixture on 4 of the tortillas. Sprinkle each with a quarter
of the cheese and top with another tortilla.

Heat the remaining oil in a non-stick frying pan/skillet set
over medium heat. When hot, add a quesadilla, lower the heat
and cook for 2–3 minutes until golden on one side and the
cheese begins to melt. Turn over and cook the other side for
2–3 minutes. Transfer to a heatproof plate and keep warm in
the preheated oven while you cook the rest.

To serve, top each quesadilla with sour cream, spring onions/
scallions, diced tomatoes and sliced olives. Cut into wedges
and serve immediately.

These breakfast quesadillas are a complete departure from traditional Mexican ingredients. If you want to make them more authentic, replace the baked beans with refried beans.

# Ham & egg breakfast quesadilla with baked beans

. . . . . . . . . . . . . . . . . . . .

4 thick slices ham
8 large flour tortillas
200 g/2 cups grated Cheddar
   or Monterey Jack cheese
400-g/14-oz. can baked beans
   in tomato sauce
1 tablespoon vegetable oil
4 tablespoons unsalted butter
4 large eggs

**SERVES 4–6**

Preheat the oven to 120°C (250°F) Gas ½.

To assemble the quesadillas, put 1 slice of ham on 4 of the tortillas. Sprinkle each with a quarter of the cheese and spoon over a quarter of the beans. Top with another tortilla.

Heat the oil in a non-stick frying pan/skillet set over medium heat. When hot, add a quesadilla, lower the heat and cook for 2–3 minutes until golden on one side and the cheese begins to melt. Turn over and cook the other side for 2–3 minutes. Transfer to a heatproof plate and keep warm in the preheated oven while you cook the rest.

Melt 1 tablespoon of the butter in a small non-stick frying pan/skillet. Add 1 egg and fry until cooked through, turning once to cook both sides if desired. Repeat to cook the remaining eggs.

To serve, top each quesadilla with a fried egg. Cut into wedges and serve immediately.

Serve these for brunch, lunch or dinner, with rice and beans if a more substantial meal is required. The chicken can be prepared in advance to make this recipe even more speedy.

# Chicken & chorizo quesadilla

. . . . . . . . . . . . . . . . . . . .

650 g/1 lb 7 oz. boneless, skinless chicken
chicken or vegetable stock, or water, as required
2 tablespoons vegetable oil
1 onion, finely chopped
2 garlic cloves, finely chopped
1 teaspoon ground cumin
1 teaspoon dried oregano
1 teaspoon fine sea salt
1 fresh green chilli/chile, finely chopped
70 g/2 oz. chorizo, finely chopped
400-g/14-oz. can chopped tomatoes
8 large flour tortillas
200 g/2 cups grated Cheddar or Monterey Jack cheese

**TO SERVE**
sour cream
Guacamole (see page 60)

**SERVES 4–6**

Preheat the oven to 120°C (250°F) Gas ½.

Put the chicken in a saucepan and add enough stock or water to cover. If using water or unseasoned stock, season with salt. Bring to the boil over medium heat, then cover and simmer for 30–40 minutes until cooked through. Remove from the pan and let cool, then shred the chicken using your hands or two forks. Taste and adjust the seasoning.

Heat 1 tablespoon of the oil in a saucepan over medium–high heat. Add the onion and cook for 5–8 minutes, stirring occasionally, until golden. Add the garlic, cumin, oregano, salt, chilli/chile and chorizo and cook for 1–2 minutes, stirring often. Stir in the tomatoes and cover. Simmer for 15 minutes then uncover and cook for 10–20 minutes until reduced.

To assemble the quesadillas, spread a quarter of the chicken mixture on 4 of the tortillas. Sprinkle each with a quarter of the cheese and top with another tortilla.

Heat the remaining oil in a non-stick frying pan/skillet set over medium heat. When hot, add a quesadilla, lower the heat and cook for 2–3 minutes until golden on one side and the cheese begins to melt. Turn over and cook the other side for 2–3 minutes. Transfer to a heatproof plate and keep warm in the preheated oven while you cook the rest.

To serve, top each quesadilla with sour cream and Guacamole. Cut into wedges and serve immediately.

In this delicious recipe, the sweetness of the potatoes is perfectly complemented by the salty tang of the cheese and the smoky flavour of the chipotle chillies/chiles.

# Sweet potato, spinach & goat cheese quesadilla

........................

800 g/1 lb 12 oz. sweet potatoes, cut into chunks
1 large chipotle chilli/chile in adobo sauce, finely chopped plus 1 teaspoon of adobo sauce
1 teaspoon fine sea salt
200 g/3½ cups fresh spinach
8 large flour tortillas
150-g/5½-oz. log of goat cheese, thinly sliced
vegetable oil

**TO SERVE**
sour cream
Guacamole (see page 60)
sprigs of fresh coriander/cilantro
lemon wedges

**SERVES 4–6**

Preheat the oven to 120°C (250°F) Gas ½.

Boil, steam or roast the sweet potatoes until tender and leave to cool. When cool, mash the flesh with the chilli/chile and salt. Taste and adjust the seasoning and set aside. Put the spinach in a large saucepan, cover and set over low heat just to wilt. Allow to cool, then squeeze out any excess moisture from the cooked spinach using your hands. Chop finely and set aside until needed.

To assemble the quesadillas, spread 2–3 tablespoons of sweet potato purée on 4 of the tortillas. Dot the spinach evenly over the surface and add a quarter of the cheese slices. Top with another tortilla.

Heat the remaining oil in a non-stick frying pan/skillet set over medium heat. When hot, add a quesadilla, lower the heat and cook for 2–3 minutes until golden on one side and the cheese begins to melt. Turn over and cook the other side for 2–3 minutes. Transfer to a heatproof plate and keep warm in the preheated oven while you cook the rest.

To serve, top each quesadilla with sour cream and Guacamole. Cut into wedges, top with sprigs of coriander/cilantro and serve immediately with lemon wedges for squeezing.

The smoky taste of chipotle is irresistible mixed with the warmth of the cinnamon and the salty tang of the cheese. For an authentic Mexican taste, replace the feta with queso fresco.

# Chipotle, black bean & feta quesadilla

· · · · · · · · · · · · · · · · · · · ·

3 tablespoons vegetable oil

1 onion, diced

3 garlic cloves, crushed

1 teaspoon dried oregano

1 teaspoon ground cumin

a pinch of ground cinnamon

2 chipotle chillies/chiles in adobo sauce, finely chopped

200 g/1 cup passata (Italian sieved tomatoes)

2 x 400-g/14-oz. can black beans, drained

fine sea salt

8 large flour tortillas

200 g/2 cups feta cheese or queso fresco, crumbled

sour cream, to serve

Pico de Gallo (see page 63), to serve

SERVES 4–6

Preheat the oven to 120°C (250°F) Gas ½.

Heat 2 tablespoons of the oil in a saucepan set over medium–high heat. Add the onion and cook for 5–8 minutes, stirring occasionally, until golden. Add the garlic, oregano, cumin and cinnamon and cook for 1–2 minutes, stirring often. Add the chopped chillies/chiles and cook for 1 minute further, stirring often. Stir in the passata, beans, a pinch of salt and 60 ml/¼ cup water and cover. Simmer for 15 minutes then taste and adjust the seasoning.

To assemble the quesadillas, spread a quarter of the bean mixture on 4 of the tortillas. Sprinkle each with a quarter of the cheese and top with another tortilla.

Heat the remaining oil in a non-stick frying pan/skillet set over medium heat. When hot, add a quesadilla, lower the heat and cook for 2–3 minutes until golden on one side and the cheese begins to melt. Turn over and cook the other side for 2–3 minutes. Transfer to a heatproof plate and keep warm in the preheated oven while you cook the rest.

To serve, top each quesadilla with sour cream and Pico de Gallo. Cut into wedges and serve immediately.

Prawns/shrimp and avocados are soul mates in many cuisines, but here they are given an authentic Mexican flavour with some spicy jalapeños. Serve this on its own, or accompany with a tomato salad for a more substantial meal.

# Seafood & avocado quesadilla

. . . . . . . . . . . . . . . . . . . .

2 large ripe avocados, coarsely chopped
a pinch of fine sea salt
juice of ½ lemon
a small bunch of chopped fresh coriander/cilantro
500 g/1 lb 2 oz. cooked prawns/shrimp, shelled
8 large flour tortillas
2 large tomatoes, coarsely chopped
150 g/5½ oz. firm goat cheese, grated or thinly sliced
4 tablespoon pickled jalapeños, sliced
1 tablespoon vegetable oil
lemon wedges, to serve

**SERVES 4**

Preheat the oven to 120°C (250°F) Gas ½.

Put the avocados in a bowl, season lightly with salt and add the lemon juice and coriander/cilantro. Toss to combine and set aside.

If the prawns/shrimp are very large, cut them in half.

To assemble the quesadillas, put a quarter of the prawns/shrimp on 4 of the tortillas. Sprinkle each with a quarter of the chopped avocados, tomatoes and cheese and 1 tablespoon of jalapeños. Top with another tortilla.

Heat the oil in a non-stick frying pan/skillet set over medium heat. When hot, add a quesadilla, lower the heat and cook for 2–3 minutes until golden on one side and the cheese begins to melt. Turn over and cook the other side for 2–3 minutes. Transfer to a heatproof plate and keep warm in the preheated oven while you cook the rest.

To serve, cut the quesadillas into wedges and serve immediately with lemon wedges on the side for squeezing.

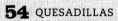

This beautifully simple recipe is ideal for a snack to serve with drinks before a more substantial Mexican-style meal. It is also good for breakfast, served with a fried egg or two on top.

# Cheese, tomato & jalapeño quesadilla

· · · · · · · · · · · · · · · · · · · ·

4–5 ripe tomatoes, thinly sliced
8 large flour tortillas
300 g/3 cups grated Cheddar
   or Monterey Jack cheese
80–100 g/½ cup pickled jalapeños,
   chopped
1 tablespoon vegetable oil
Guacamole (see page 60), to serve

**SERVES 4**

Preheat the oven to 120°C (250°F) Gas ½.

To assemble the quesadillas, put a quarter of the tomato slices on 4 of the tortillas. Sprinkle each with a quarter of the cheese and jalapeños. Top with another tortilla.

Heat the oil in a non-stick frying pan/skillet set over medium heat. When hot, add a quesadilla, lower the heat and cook for 2–3 minutes until golden on one side and the cheese begins to melt. Turn over and cook the other side for 2–3 minutes. Transfer to a heatproof plate and keep warm in the preheated oven while you cook the rest.

To serve, cut the quesadillas into wedges and serve immediately with Guacamole on the side.

# Sides & salsas

Tasty seasoned rice makes a really great accompaniment to any taco or quesadilla.

# Red rice

. . . . . . . . . . . . . . . . . . . . . .

1 tablespoon vegetable oil
1 small onion, finely chopped
400 g/2 cups short grain white rice
1½ teaspoons ground cumin
½ teaspoon ancho chilli/chili powder
1 generous teaspoon dried oregano
1 generous teaspoon fine sea salt
1 teaspoon dried chilli/hot pepper flakes (optional)
2 tablespoons tomato purée/paste

**SERVES 4–6**

Heat the oil in a large saucepan set over medium-high heat. Add the onion and cook for 5 minutes until golden.

Stir in the rice, cumin, chilli/chili powder, oregano, salt and dried chilli/hot pepper flakes, if using, and cook for 2–3 minutes.

Add 800 ml/3 cups water and the tomato purée/paste and stir just to blend. Bring to the boil, then lower the heat, cover and simmer for about 20 minutes, or until all the water has been absorbed.

Fluff with a fork and serve immediately.

This crunchy slaw is the traditional topping for fish tacos.

# Baja slaw

. . . . . . . . . . . . . . . . . . . . . .

4 tablespoons mayonnaise
1 tablespoon lime juice
1 teaspoon fine sea salt
a dash of hot sauce (such as Tabasco)
a pinch of ground cumin
1 small white cabbage, thinly sliced
1 small bunch of radishes, thinly sliced
a small bunch of fresh coriander/cilantro,
    finely chopped

**SERVES 4–6**

Put the mayonnaise, lime juice, salt, Tabasco and cumin in a large bowl and mix well.

Add the sliced cabbage, radishes and coriander/cilantro and toss to combine. Taste and adjust the seasoning and chill until needed.

These authentic beans have a deliciously smoky flavour.

# Mexican-style beans

· · · · · · · · · · · · · · · · · · · · ·

4 garlic cloves, unpeeled
4 plum tomatoes, chopped
1 chipotle chilli/chile in adobo
    sauce
½ teaspoon ground cumin
2 x 400-g/14-oz. cans black
    or pinto beans, drained
2 tablespoons vegetable oil
fine sea salt

**SERVES 6–8**

Heat a stovetop grill pan/griddle until hot. Cook the garlic and tomatoes over high heat for 3–5 minutes until charred and leave to cool. When cool, slip the garlic cloves out of their skins. Put the garlic, tomatoes, chilli/chile, cumin and beans in a blender and work to a coarse purée.

Heat the oil in a saucepan over medium heat. Add the beans and cook for 15–20 minutes, stirring often, until thick. Taste and adjust the seasoning. Serve hot.

I like to keep it simple so this is the purist's recipe.

# Guacamole

· · · · · · · · · · · · · · · · · · · · ·

2 ripe avocados, chopped
2–3 tablespoons sour cream
juice of ½ lemon
a small bunch of fresh coriander/
    cilantro, finely chopped
a pinch of ground cumin
½ teaspoon fine sea salt
1 small fresh chilli/chile, green
    or red, (optional)

**SERVES 4–6**

Put the avocados in a small bowl and mash to a coarse paste using a fork.

Stir in the sour cream, lemon juice, coriander/cilantro, cumin, salt and chilli/chile if using. Mix well. Taste and adjust the seasoning, adding more salt or lemon juice, as desired.

This delicious salsa works with almost any taco filling.

# Roasted tomato salsa

· · · · · · · · · · · · · · · · · · · · ·

950 g/2 lbs 2 oz. ripe tomatoes
1 large onion, thickly sliced
4 fresh green chillies/chiles
a small bunch of fresh
    coriander/cilantro
fine sea salt
a pinch of sugar
2 tablespoons lime juice

**SERVES 4–6**

Heat a stovetop grill pan/griddle over high heat. Add the tomatoes, onion and chillies/chiles and cook for 3–5 minutes on each side until charred all over.

Put the onion, tomatoes, chillies/chiles, and coriander/cilantro in a blender and work to a coarse purée. Transfer to a bowl and stir in the salt, sugar and lime juice. Chill until needed, then serve at room temperature.

This tangy salsa is best with chicken or vegetable fillings.

# Sweetcorn-lime salsa

. . . . . . . . . . . . . . . . . . . .

3 corn cobs, cooked
1 small red onion, finely chopped
1 red bell pepper, finely chopped
1 fresh red chilli/chile, finely
    chopped
1 bunch fresh coriander/cilantro
juice and zest of 1 lime
½ teaspoon fine sea salt

**SERVES 4–6**

Scrape the corn kernels into a bowl. Add the onion, pepper, chilli/chile, coriander/cilantro and the lime juice and zest and salt and toss well.

Let stand for at least 1 hour or cover and chill overnight. Taste and adjust the seasoning, adding more chilli/chile or lime juice if desired. Chill until needed, then serve at room temperature.

Add a splash of colour with bright green tomatillo salsa.

# Tomatillo salsa

. . . . . . . . . . . . . . . . . . . .

2 fresh green chillies/chiles
3–4 garlic cloves, unpeeled
800 g/4 cups canned tomatillos,
    drained
1 small onion
1 small bunch of fresh
    coriander/cilantro
a pinch of sugar

**SERVES 4–6**

Heat a stovetop grill pan/griddle until hot. Cook the chillies/chiles and garlic for 3–5 minutes until charred and leave to cool. When cool, slip the garlic cloves out of their skins.

Combine the tomatillos, garlic, chillies/chiles, onion and coriander/cilantro in a blender and process to a coarse purée. Transfer to a bowl and stir in the sugar. Taste and adjust the seasoning. Chill until needed, then serve at room temperature.

Pico de Gallo is so tasty, it can be a filling on its own.

# Pico de gallo

. . . . . . . . . . . . . . . . . . . .

6–8 ripe tomatoes
1 large red onion, finely chopped
1 fresh green chilli/chile, or more
    to taste, finely chopped
1 bunch fresh coriander/cilantro
½ teaspoon fine sea salt
juice of 1 lime
lemon juice, optional

**SERVES 4–6**

Put the tomatoes, onion, chilli/chile and coriander/cilantro in a small bowl. Add the salt and lime juice and toss well.

Let stand for at least 1 hour or cover and refrigerate overnight. Taste and adjust the seasoning, adding more chilli/chile or a squeeze of lemon juice if desired. Chill until needed, then serve at room temperature.

# Index